TAGAKI
多書き

TAGAKI（多書き）とは、一言で言えば、「英語で自分を表現することを学ぶための、ボルダリング競技みたいなもの」です。その足場はメンタル面と英語面の2種類で、この足場を使って登って行き頂上を目指しましょう。このTAGAKIでは、考える→書く→伝えるを30トピックくり返すことで、自分の意見を持ち、英語を書けるようになります。そうすると世界に飛び出して行けそうな自分を感じることができるでしょう。

TAGAKI 10 ✏️ Contents もくじ

このワークブックの進め方		4

Topics	**Categories**	
1 **Aquariums** (水族館)	Living Things	6
2 **Athletics** (いろいろな運動)	Sport	8
3 **Ball Sports** (ボールを使ったスポーツ)	Sport	10
4 **Barbeques** (バーベキュー)	Food	12
5 **Bread** (パン)	Food	14
6 **Cats** (ネコ)	Living Things	16
7 **Cleaning** (掃除)	School Life	18
8 **Cool Japan** (日本のほこり)	Society	20
9 **Dinner** (夕食)	Food	22
10 **Dogs** (犬)	Living Things	24
11 **Endangered Species** (絶滅危惧種)	Living Things	26
12 **Family Members** (家族について)	Personality	28
13 **Fashion** (ファッション)	Fashion	30
14 **If I Get One Million Yen ...** (もし100万円もらったら…)	Personality	32
15 **Interests** (興味を持っていること)	Personality	34
16 **Japanese Foods** (日本食)	Food	36
17 **Jam** (ジャム)	Food	38
18 **Locations** (ロケーション)	Places	40
19 **Meals** (食事)	Food	42
20 **Musical Instruments** (楽器)	Music	44
21 **Past** (昔)	Personality	46

22	**Reading and Writing**（読んだり書いたりするもの）	Personality	48
23	**Reptiles and Amphibians**（爬虫類と両生類）	Living Things	50
24	**Saturday**（土曜日）	Personality	52
25	**School Lunch**（給食）	School Life	54
26	**Sneaker Colors**（スニーカーの色）	Fashion	56
27	**Sports Day**（運動会）	School Life	58
28	**Taste**（味覚）	Food	60
29	**Vending Machines**（自動販売機）	Society	62
30	**World Heritage Sites**（世界遺産）	Places	64

進度表 終わったトピックの番号に印をつけていきましょう！

TAGAKI 10 をはじめよう

英語を書くのに慣れていない人は、初めの5回を過ぎたら楽に書けるようになるのでがんばりましょう。書くのに慣れている人は、機械的に書くのではなく、自分の言いたいことについて常に想像力を働かせて書いてみましょう。そして書いた文を音声にすることに慣れていきましょう。

進め方

Step 1 Thinking / Reading

トピックについて考えましょう。
Sample Sentences A B C の文を読みましょう。
Words and Phrases 1〜12 のイラストを見てなるべく早くどれを書くか自分の心を決めましょう。

Step 2 Listening

Sample Sentences と Words and Phrases の音声をQRコードできくことができます。音声をチェックしましょう。

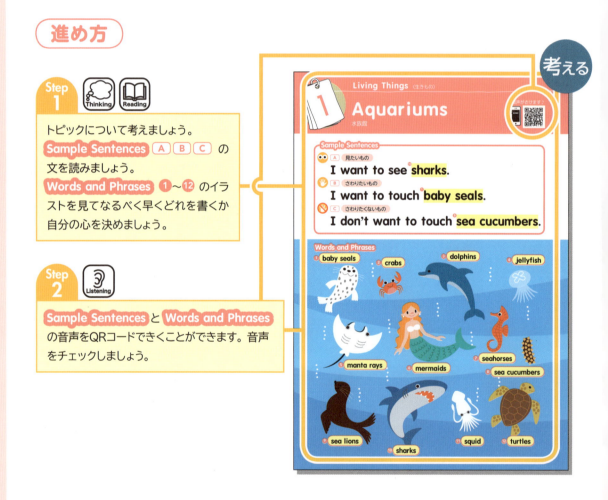

1人でTAGAKIを学ぶ人へ

単独の良さをいかし、自由に自分のペースでStep 1〜5を進んでください。自分で自分の進歩を見届け、それぞれの目的や目標、例えば入試や検定試験、会議やプレゼンなどのために書く力を付けてください。

TAGAKI 10 目標

メンタル	自分の気持ちを即断即決する

自分の気持ちを決めることが大きな目標です。30トピックについて、自分の気持ちを短時間で整理整頓し、表現できるようになることが大切です。

英語	10語前後の英文をたくさん書く

英語を使用する世界の人びとがよく使う慣用表現を単語ベースではなく、10words前後の英文で表現しましょう。

書く 3～5分で書きましょう。

Step 3 Writing

Sample Sentences A B C の黄色の部分を Words and Phrases ①～⑫ から自分で選んだものに入れかえて、それぞれ2つずつ6つの文を全文、書き写しましょう。

Step 4 Writing

Writing Time ❶ で書いた A B C の文を1つずつ選んで、今度は見ないで書きましょう。

伝える

Step 5 Speaking

Writing Time ❷ で書いた文を覚えて声に出して言いましょう。

ペアやグループでTAGAKIを学ぶ人へ	Step 1～5を進めた後、友達や家族、先生に向けて発表したり、他の人の発表を聞いて、英語または日本語でディスカッションしたりして、4技能の学習へ発展してください。書いたものは見ないで発表しましょう。

5

Living Things 〈生きもの〉

Aquariums
水族館

Sample Sentences

A 見たいもの
I want to see ¹⁰sharks.

B さわりたいもの
I want to touch ¹baby seals.

C さわりたくないもの
I don't want to touch ⁸sea cucumbers.

Words and Phrases

1. baby seals
2. crabs
3. dolphins
4. jellyfish
5. manta rays
6. mermaids
7. seahorses
8. sea cucumbers
9. sea lions
10. sharks
11. squid
12. turtles

Writing Time

1　　　　　の単語を入れかえて、 A B C の全文を 2 つずつ書こう。

A

B

C

2 上で書いた文を 1 つずつ選んで見ないで書き、見ないで言おう。

A

B

C

2 Sport 〈スポーツ〉
Athletics
いろいろな運動

Sample Sentences

 A 得意な運動
I'm good at **handstands**.

 B 苦手な運動
I'm not good at **long-distance running**.

 C 挑戦してみたい運動
I want to try **triple twists**.

Words and Phrases

① triple twists

② backflips

③ backward rolls

④ cartwheels

⑤ forward rolls

⑥ handstands

⑦ pullovers

⑧ jumping rope

⑨ long-distance running

⑩ push-ups

⑪ sprinting

⑫ standing on one leg

TAGAKI 10

Writing Time

1 ⬛ ▭ の単語を入れかえて、Ａ Ｂ Ｃ の全文を 2 つずつ書こう。

😊 Ａ

😖 Ｂ

💪 Ｃ

2 上で書いた文を 1 つずつ選んで見ないで書き、見ないで言おう。

😊 Ａ

😖 Ｂ

💪 Ｃ

9

3 Sport 〈スポーツ〉
Ball Sports
ボールを使ったスポーツ

Sample Sentences

 A 自分がするボールスポーツ
I play table tennis.

 B 自分がしないボールスポーツ
I don't play golf.

 C 自分がやってみたいボールスポーツ
I want to try slamball.

Words and Phrases

① baseball

② basketball

③ beach volleyball

④ cricket

⑤ dodgeball

⑥ golf

⑦ rugby

⑧ slamball

⑨ soccer

⑩ table tennis

⑪ tennis

⑫ volleyball

10

TAGAKI 10

Writing Time

1 🟨 の単語を入れかえて、 A B C の全文を２つずつ書こう。

⚾ A

🚫 B

🐾 C

2 上で書いた文を１つずつ選んで見ないで書き、見ないで言おう。

⚾ A

🚫 B

🐾 C

11

4 Food 〈食べもの〉
Barbeques
バーベキュー

音声がきけます♪

Sample Sentences

A 家族で焼くもの
We cook rice balls on the barbeque.

B 家族で焼かないもの
We don't cook bananas on the barbeque.

C 自分が焼きたいもの
I want to cook beef on the barbeque.

Words and Phrases

1. bananas
2. chicken
3. eggplants
4. fish
5. green peppers
6. onions
7. pork
8. rice balls
9. sausages
10. shrimp
11. beef
12. tomatoes

TAGAKI 10

Writing Time

1 ⬚ の単語を入れかえて、 A B C の全文を2つずつ書こう。

A

B

C

2 上で書いた文を1つずつ選んで見ないで書き、見ないで言おう。

A

B

C

13

Food 〈食べもの〉
Bread
パン

Sample Sentences

A 朝食に食べたいパン
I want to eat ³croissants for breakfast.

B 昼食に買いたいパン
I want to buy ²corn buns for lunch.

C 毎朝食べたくないパン
I don't want to eat ¹⁰raisin bread every morning.

Words and Phrases

 1. chocolate bread
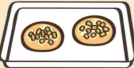 2. corn buns
 3. croissants
 4. curry buns

 5. custard buns
 6. French toast
 7. ham and cheese bread
 8. hot dogs

9. melon buns
10. raisin bread
11. red bean buns
12. sugar rolls

TAGAKI 10

Writing Time

1 ▢▢▢▢ の単語を入れかえて、 A B C の全文を 2 つずつ書こう。

A

B

C

2 上で書いた文を 1 つずつ選んで見ないで書き、見ないで言おう。

A

B

C

15

Living Things 〈生きもの〉

Cats
ネコ

音声がきけます♪

Sample Sentences

💗 A　ネコが好きな理由
I like cats, because they're ⑥**independent**.

💔 B　ネコが好きではない理由
I don't like cats, because they're ⑧**noisy**.

💭 C　ネコについて思うこと
I think that cats are ⑩**selfish**.

Words and Phrases

1. beautiful
2. clean
3. curious
4. cute
5. funny
6. independent
7. noble
8. noisy
9. playful
10. selfish
11. soft
12. warm

16

TAGAKI 10

Writing Time

1 　 の単語を入れかえて、 A B C の全文を 2 つずつ書こう。

A

B

C

2 上で書いた文を 1 つずつ選んで見ないで書き、見ないで言おう。

A

B

C

17

1 Cleaning
School Life 〈学校生活〉
掃除

音声がきけます♪

Sample Sentences

 A いつも掃除する場所
We always clean ³the floors.

 B 時どき掃除する場所
We sometimes clean ⁹the music room.

 C 掃除したくない場所
We don't want to clean ⁶the toilets.

Words and Phrases

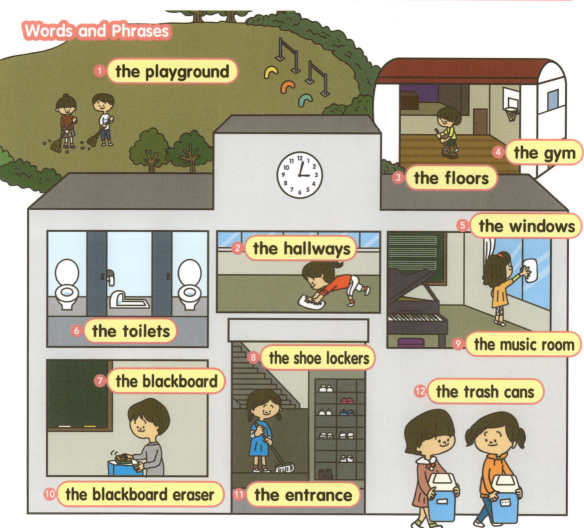

1. the playground
2. the hallways
3. the floors
4. the gym
5. the windows
6. the toilets
7. the blackboard
8. the shoe lockers
9. the music room
10. the blackboard eraser
11. the entrance
12. the trash cans

18

TAGAKI 10

Writing Time

1 ＿＿＿＿ の単語を入れかえて、Ⓐ Ⓑ Ⓒ の全文を 2 つずつ書こう。

✉ Ⓐ

✉ Ⓑ

✉ Ⓒ

2 上で書いた文を 1 つずつ選んで見ないで書き、見ないで言おう。

✉ Ⓐ

✉ Ⓑ

✉ Ⓒ

19

Society 〈社会〉
Cool Japan
日本のほこり

Sample Sentences

 A 自分がほこりに思うこと
I'm proud of ⁽¹⁰⁾ **the polite people**.

 B 自分が心配していること
I'm worried about ⁽¹¹⁾ **the safety**.

 C 日本人みんながほこりに思うこと
We're proud of ⁽²⁾ **the clean streets**.

Words and Phrases

① everything being on time　② the clean streets　③ the clean water　④ the crowded trains

 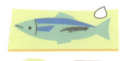 

⑤ the good service　⑥ the healthy food　⑦ the Internet　⑧ the public transport

⑨ the old shrines and temples　⑩ the polite people　⑪ the safety　⑫ the tasty food

TAGAKI 10

Writing Time

1 　　　　 の単語を入れかえて、 A B C の全文を 2 つずつ書こう。

😁 A

🏞 B

🔴 C

2 上で書いた文を 1 つずつ選んで見ないで書き、見ないで言おう。

😁 A

🏞 B

🔴 C

21

Food 〈食べもの〉

Dinner
夕食

音声がきけます♪

Sample Sentences

A 今晩の夕食に食べたいもの
I want ⑪**sukiyaki** for dinner tonight.

B 今晩の夕食に食べたくないもの
I don't want ⑧**sandwiches** for dinner tonight.

C 毎日食べたいもの
I wish I had ⑫**sushi** every day.

Words and Phrases

① chicken and egg bowls

② fried rice

③ Korean barbeque (yakiniku)

④ pizza

⑤ pot stickers (gyoza)

⑥ ramen

⑦ salad

⑧ sandwiches

⑨ spaghetti

⑩ spring rolls

⑪ sukiyaki

⑫ sushi

22

TAGAKI 10

Writing Time

1 　　　　　の単語を入れかえて、A B C の全文を 2 つずつ書こう。

A

B

C

2 上で書いた文を 1 つずつ選んで見ないで書き、見ないで言おう。

A

B

C

23

10 Living Things 〈生きもの〉
Dogs
犬

音声がきけます♪

Sample Sentences

💗 A 飼いたい犬
I want to have a ⑫**smart** dog.

💔 B 飼いたくない犬
I don't want to have a ⑧**naughty** dog.

💭 C 犬について思うこと
I think that dogs are ⑦**lovely**.

Words and Phrases

① brave
② charming
③ cool
④ cute
⑤ gentle
⑥ greedy
⑦ lovely
⑧ naughty
⑨ nervous
⑩ noisy
⑪ peaceful
⑫ smart

TAGAKI 10

Writing Time

1 ░░░░░░ の単語を入れかえて、 A B C の全文を2つずつ書こう。

♥ A

💔 B

💭 C

2 上で書いた文を1つずつ選んで見ないで書き、見ないで言おう。

♥ A

💔 B

💭 C

25

11 Living Things 〈生きもの〉

Endangered Species
絶滅危惧種

音声がきけます♪

Sample Sentences

A 自分が心配している絶滅危惧種
I'm worried about the mountain gorillas.

B 多くの人が心配している絶滅危惧種
Many people are worried about the giant pandas.

C 自分が見たことがある絶滅危惧種
I've seen the chimpanzees.

Words and Phrases

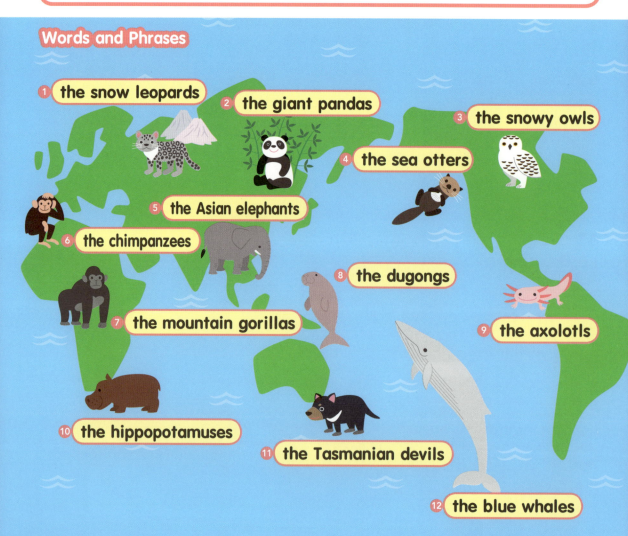

1. the snow leopards
2. the giant pandas
3. the snowy owls
4. the sea otters
5. the Asian elephants
6. the chimpanzees
7. the mountain gorillas
8. the dugongs
9. the axolotls
10. the hippopotamuses
11. the Tasmanian devils
12. the blue whales

26

TAGAKI 10

Writing Time

1 　　　　　 の単語を入れかえて、 A B C の全文を2つずつ書こう。

A

B

C

2 上で書いた文を1つずつ選んで見ないで書き、見ないで言おう。

A

B

C

27

Personality 〈パーソナリティー〉

Family Members
家族について

Sample Sentences

 A　私の姉／妹が楽しむこと
My sister enjoys taking a bath.⑪

 B　私のおばあさんが好きなこと
My grandma likes singing.⑩

 C　飼っている犬が大好きなこと
Our dog loves taking a nap.⑫

家族：dad お父さん、mom お母さん、brother 兄／弟、sister 姉／妹、grandpa おじいさん、grandma おばあさん

Words and Phrases

① cooking

② dancing

③ driving

④ fishing

⑤ playing games

⑥ playing shogi

⑦ playing the piano

⑧ practicing calligraphy

⑨ relaxing on the sofa

⑩ singing

⑪ taking a bath

⑫ taking a nap

TAGAKI 10

Writing Time

1 □□□□□ の単語を入れかえて、A B C の全文を2つずつ書こう。
□□□□□ をほかの家族にかえて書いてもよいです。

A

B

C

2 上で書いた文を1つずつ選んで見ないで書き、見ないで言おう。

A

B

C

29

Fashion 〈ファッション〉

Sample Sentences

 A やってみたいファッション
I want to try a crazy wig.[5]

 B やってみたくないファッション
I don't want to try a topknot.[12]

 C やったことがないファッション
I haven't tried colorful nails.[4]

Words and Phrases

① pierced ears

② big rings

③ blonde hair

④ colorful nails

⑤ a crazy wig

⑥ false eyelashes

⑦ high-heeled shoes

⑧ jeans with holes

⑨ long skirts

⑩ necklaces

⑪ permed hair

⑫ a topknot
(samurai hairstyle)

TAGAKI 10

Writing Time

1 　　　　　　の単語を入れかえて、 A B C の全文を 2 つずつ書こう。

A

B

C

2 上で書いた文を 1 つずつ選んで見ないで書き、見ないで言おう。

A

B

C

31

14 Personality 〈パーソナリティー〉

If I Get One Million Yen ...
もし100万円もらったら…

音声がきけます♪

Sample Sentences

A　もし100万円もらったらすること
I'll buy all the games.

B　もし100万円もらってもしないこと
I won't save the money.

C　もし100万円もらったらするべきこと
I should give it to my mom and dad.

Words and Phrases

① build a tree house

② buy a car

③ buy a dog

④ buy all the games

⑤ buy lottery tickets

⑥ donate it

⑦ give it to my mom and dad

⑧ go on a cruise

⑨ go overseas

⑩ have parties

⑪ save the money

⑫ stay at a luxury hotel

TAGAKI 10

Writing Time

1 _____ の単語を入れかえて、 A B C の全文を 2 つずつ書こう。

A

B

C

2 上で書いた文を 1 つずつ選んで見ないで書き、見ないで言おう。

A

B

C

33

Personality 〈パーソナリティー〉

Interests
興味を持っていること

音声がきけます♪

Sample Sentences

A 興味を持っていること
I'm interested in movie stars.

B 興味を持っていないこと
I'm not interested in the Internet.

C 全く知らないこと
I have no idea about sports.

Words and Phrases

① artists

② comic books

③ fashion

④ friends' romances

⑤ Japanese history

⑥ money

⑦ movie stars

⑧ politics and economics

⑨ sports

⑩ the Internet

⑪ video games

⑫ World Heritage Sites

TAGAKI 10

Writing Time

1 　　　　　　の単語を入れかえて、 A B C の全文を 2 つずつ書こう。

💚 A

💔 B

🚫 C

2 上で書いた文を 1 つずつ選んで見ないで書き、見ないで言おう。

💚 A

💚 B

🚫 C

35

16 Food 〈食べもの〉
Japanese Foods
日本食

Sample Sentences

 A 観光客に食べてほしいもの
I want tourists to eat takoyaki.

 B 観光客におすすめのもの
I recommend gyudon.

 C 観光客におすすめしないもの
I don't recommend ika no shiokara.

Words and Phrases

1. edamame (green soybeans)
2. gyudon (beef bowls)
3. katsudon (pork cutlet bowls)
4. manju (steamed buns with red bean paste)
5. natto (fermented soybeans)
6. ika no shiokara (salted fermented squid)
7. somen (thin wheat noodles)
8. takoyaki (octopus dumplings)
9. umeboshi (pickled plums)
10. tempura (battered deep-fried fish and vegetables)
11. udon (thick wheat noodles)
12. yudofu (boiled tofu)

TAGAKI 10

Writing Time

1 　　　　　の単語を入れかえて、 A B C の全文を２つずつ書こう。

A

B

C

2 上で書いた文を１つずつ選んで見ないで書き、見ないで言おう。

A

B

C

37

17

Food 〈食べもの〉

Jam
ジャム

音声がきけます♪

Sample Sentences

A　よく食べるジャム
I often eat **raspberry** jam.

B　ヨーグルトといっしょに時どき食べるジャム
I sometimes eat **blueberry** jam with yogurt.

C　食べたことがないジャム
I've never eaten **lemon** jam.

Words and Phrases

 1 apricot
 2 blueberry
 3 cranberry
 4 grape

 5 lemon
 6 mango
 7 melon
 8 orange

 9 peach
 10 pineapple
 11 raspberry
 12 strawberry

TAGAKI 10

Writing Time

1 ▢ 　　　　の単語を入れかえて、 A B C の全文を 2 つずつ書こう。

A

B

C

2 上で書いた文を 1 つずつ選んで見ないで書き、見ないで言おう。

A

B

C

39

18 Places 〈場所〉

Locations
ロケーション

 音声がきけます♪

Sample Sentences

 A 家の近くにあるもの
There's a park near my house.

 B 家から遠くにあるもの
There's a shopping mall far from my house.

 C 家の近くにあってほしいもの
I want a dog park near my house.

Words and Phrases

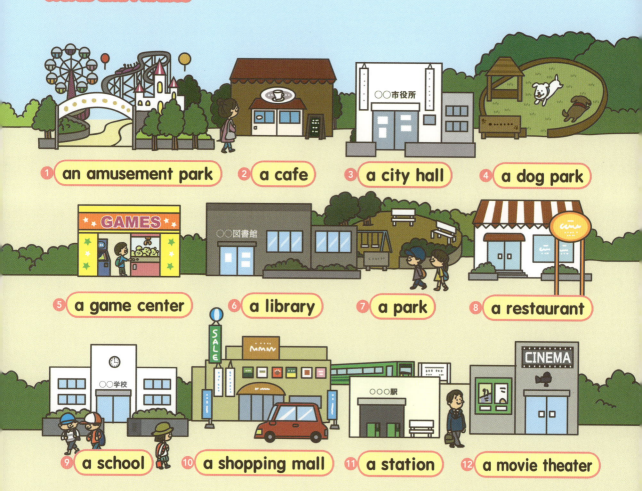

1. an amusement park
2. a cafe
3. a city hall
4. a dog park
5. a game center
6. a library
7. a park
8. a restaurant
9. a school
10. a shopping mall
11. a station
12. a movie theater

40

TAGAKI 10

Writing Time

1 ＿＿＿＿ の単語を入れかえて、 A B C の全文を 2 つずつ書こう。

A

B

C

2 上で書いた文を 1 つずつ選んで見ないで書き、見ないで言おう。

A

B

C

41

19 Food 〈食べもの〉
Meals
食事

Sample Sentences

A　いつも食べている食事
I usually have a simple meal.

B　時どき食べたい食事
I sometimes want a gorgeous meal.

C　お気に入りの食事
My favorite meal is a healthy meal.

Words and Phrases

 ① cheap

 ② fast

 ③ formal

 ④ good

⑤ gorgeous

⑥ healthy

⑦ heavy

⑧ light

 ⑨ satisfying

 ⑩ simple

⑪ stand-up

 ⑫ surprising

42

TAGAKI 10

Writing Time

1 　　　　　 の単語を入れかえて、 A B C の全文を 2 つずつ書こう。

A

B

C

2 上で書いた文を 1 つずつ選んで見ないで書き、見ないで言おう。

A

B

C

43

Music 〈音楽〉

Musical Instruments
楽器

音声がきけます♪

Sample Sentences

 A 演奏できる楽器
I can play ⁹the recorder.

 B 演奏できない楽器
I can't play ⁷the ocarina.

 C 挑戦してみたい楽器
I want to try ²the drums.

Words and Phrases

1 the clarinet
2 the drums
3 the flute
4 the horn
5 the Japanese drums
6 the koto
7 the ocarina
8 the piano
9 the recorder
10 the trombone
11 the trumpet
12 the violin

44

TAGAKI 10

Writing Time

1 　　　　　 の単語を入れかえて、 A B C の全文を 2 つずつ書こう。

A

B

C

2 上で書いた文を 1 つずつ選んで見ないで書き、見ないで言おう。

A

B

C

45

21 Personality 〈パーソナリティー〉

Past
昔

Sample Sentences

 A　赤ちゃんの時の自分
I was fat when I was a baby.

 B　子どもの時の姉／妹
My sister was active when she was a child.

 C　赤ちゃんの時の兄／弟
My brother was noisy when he was a baby.

家族：dad お父さん、mom お母さん、brother 兄／弟、sister 姉／妹、grandpa おじいさん、grandma おばあさん

Words and Phrases

1 active

2 calm

3 fat

4 gentle

5 greedy

6 naughty

7 noisy

8 pretty

9 quiet

10 selfish

11 smart

12 thin

TAGAKI 10

Writing Time

1 ▭▭▭ の単語を入れかえて、 A B C の全文を２つずつ書こう。

A

B ▭▭▭ を mom、grandma にかえて書いてもよいです。

C ▭▭▭ を dad、grandpa にかえて書いてもよいです。

2 上で書いた文を１つずつ選んで見ないで書き、見ないで言おう。

A

B

C

47

22 Reading and Writing

Personality 〈パーソナリティー〉

読んだり書いたりするもの

音声がきけます♪

Sample Sentences

 A よく読むもの
I often read ⁴fantasy.

 B よく書くもの
I often write ³emails.

 C 読んだり書いたりしないもの
I don't read or write ¹⁰novels.

Words and Phrases

① biographies

② comic books

③ emails

④ fantasy

⑤ haiku and waka

⑥ journals

⑦ letters

⑧ magazines

⑨ newspapers

⑩ novels

⑪ quotes

⑫ textbooks

TAGAKI 10

Writing Time

1 █████ の単語を入れかえて、 A B C の全文を 2 つずつ書こう。

📖 A

✏️ B

🚫 C

2 上で書いた文を 1 つずつ選んで見ないで書き、見ないで言おう。

📖 A

✏️ B

🚫 C

49

23 Living Things 〈生きもの〉

Reptiles and Amphibians
爬虫類と両生類

音声がきけます♪

Sample Sentences

A 好きな爬虫類や両生類
I like snakes.

B ペットとして飼ってみたい爬虫類や両生類
I want to keep salamanders as pets.

C ペットとして飼いたくない爬虫類や両生類
I don't want to keep alligators as pets.

Words and Phrases

1. turtles
2. geckos
3. snakes
4. lizards
5. tortoises
6. newts
7. iguanas
8. salamanders
9. chameleons
10. frogs
11. alligators
12. crocodiles

TAGAKI 10

Writing Time

1 　　　　　の単語を入れかえて、 A B C の全文を２つずつ書こう。

A

B

C

2 上で書いた文を１つずつ選んで見ないで書き、見ないで言おう。

A

B

C

51

24 Personality 〈パーソナリティー〉

Saturday
土曜日

音声がきけます♪

Sample Sentences

 A 土曜日にしたいこと
I want to **watch videos online**[12] on Saturday.

 B 土曜日にしたくないこと
I don't want to **do my homework**[4] on Saturday.

 C いつも土曜日にすること
I always[1] **check my emails** on Saturday.

Words and Phrases

① check my emails

② clean the house

③ cook/bake

④ do my homework

⑤ do nothing

⑥ go cycling

⑦ go shopping

⑧ hang out with my friends

⑨ listen to music

⑩ play games

⑪ sleep

⑫ watch videos online

TAGAKI 10

Writing Time

1 　　　　 の単語を入れかえて、 A B C の全文を２つずつ書こう。

😄 A

😣 B

😐 C

2 上で書いた文を１つずつ選んで見ないで書き、見ないで言おう。

😄 A

😣 B

😐 C

53

25 School Life 〈学校生活〉
School Lunch
給食

音声がきけます♪

Sample Sentences

A　お気に入りの給食
My favorite school lunch is ⁴curry and rice.

B　クラスで人気の給食
Our favorite school lunch is ⁵deep-fried bread.

C　リクエストしたい給食
I wish I could have ¹a buffet.

Words and Phrases

 ① a buffet
 ② beef stew
 ③ carrot salad
 ④ curry and rice

 ⑤ deep-fried bread
 ⑥ breaded deep-fried shrimp
 ⑦ French fries
 ⑧ jelly

 ⑨ hamburgers
 ⑩ breaded deep-fried pork
 ⑪ miso soup
 ⑫ potato salad

TAGAKI 10

Writing Time

1 ▭ の単語を入れかえて、 A B C の全文を 2 つずつ書こう。

A

B

C

2 上で書いた文を 1 つずつ選んで見ないで書き、見ないで言おう。

A

B

C

55

26 Fashion 〈ファッション〉
Sneaker Colors
スニーカーの色

音声がきけます♪

Sample Sentences

 A　はいているスニーカーの色
I wear ¹**black** and ⁵**gold** sneakers.

 B　はいていないスニーカーの色
I don't wear ⁷**light green** sneakers.

 C　はいてみたいスニーカーの色
I want to try ⁹**purple** and ¹¹**silver** sneakers.

Words and Phrases

❶ black　　❷ bright orange　　❸ dark blue　　❹ dark green

❺ gold　　❻ light blue　　❼ light green　　❽ pale pink

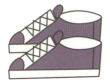   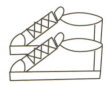

❾ purple　　❿ shocking pink　　⓫ silver　　⓬ white

56

TAGAKI 10

Writing Time

1 　　　　　の単語を入れかえて、 A B C の全文を2つずつ書こう。

A

B

C

2 上で書いた文を1つずつ選んで見ないで書き、見ないで言おう。

A

B

C

57

27 Sports Day
School Life 〈学校生活〉
運動会

音声がきけます♪

Sample Sentences

 A　みんなが好きな種目
We like ⁶the relay race.

 B　みんなが好きではない種目
We don't like ⁴the three-legged race.

 C　みんなが楽しむ種目
We enjoy ⁸the cheerleading.

Words and Phrases

1. the marching band
2. the (mock) cavalry battle
3. the obstacle race
4. the three-legged race
5. the tug of war
6. the relay race
7. the big ball race
8. the cheerleading
9. the group dancing
10. the pole pull down
11. the sprinting
12. the ball-toss game

58

TAGAKI 10

Writing Time

1 　　　　の単語を入れかえて、A B C の全文を 2 つずつ書こう。

A

B

C

2 上で書いた文を 1 つずつ選んで見ないで書き、見ないで言おう。

A

B

C

59

28 Food 〈食べもの〉
Taste
味覚

音声がきけます♪

Sample Sentences

♥ A 好きなおやつの味
I like **sweet**[12] snacks.

💔 B 好きではない味
I don't like a **sour**[9] taste.

💭 C 食べてみたい食べものの味
I want to eat **bitter**[1] food.

Words and Phrases

① bitter　② fruity　③ hot　④ mild

⑤ oily　⑥ rich　⑦ salty　⑧ sharp

⑨ sour　⑩ spicy　⑪ strange　⑫ sweet

60

Writing Time

1 ▢▢▢▢ の単語を入れかえて、 A B C の全文を 2 つずつ書こう。

💗 A

💔 B

💭 C

2 上で書いた文を 1 つずつ選んで見ないで書き、見ないで言おう。

💗 A

💔 B

💭 C

29 Society 〈社会〉

Vending Machines
自動販売機

Sample Sentences

A いつも自動販売機で買うもの
I always buy ⁶juice.

B 自動販売機で買わないもの
I don't buy ¹¹vegetables.

C 自動販売機で時どき買うもの
I sometimes buy ⁴ice cream.

Words and Phrases

1. noodles
2. eggs
3. hot tea
4. ice cream
5. iced coffee
6. juice
7. milk
8. rice
9. shampoo
10. snacks
11. vegetables
12. water

TAGAKI 10

Writing Time

1 　　　　の単語を入れかえて、A B C の全文を2つずつ書こう。

A

B

C

2 上で書いた文を1つずつ選んで見ないで書き、見ないで言おう。

A

B

C

63

30 Places〈場所〉
World Heritage Sites
世界遺産

音声がきけます♪

Sample Sentences

 A 行ったことがある世界遺産
I've been to ⁷Shiretoko.

 B 行ったことがない世界遺産
I've never been to ¹Angkor Wat.

 C いつか行ってみたい世界遺産
I want to go to ⁴Machu Picchu someday.

Words and Phrases

① Angkor Wat

② Himeji Castle

③ Horyuji Temple

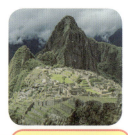
④ Machu Picchu

⑤ Mount Fuji

⑥ the Great Wall of China

⑦ Shiretoko

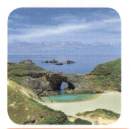
⑧ the Ogasawara Islands

⑨ the Sydney Opera House

⑩ the Tomioka Silk Mill

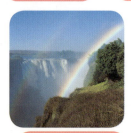
⑪ Victoria Falls

⑫ the Yaku Island

TAGAKI 10

Writing Time

1 ｜　　　　　｜の単語を入れかえて、Ⓐ Ⓑ Ⓒ の全文を 2 つずつ書こう。

Ⓐ

Ⓑ

Ⓒ

2 上で書いた文を 1 つずつ選んで見ないで書き、見ないで言おう。

Ⓐ

Ⓑ

Ⓒ

65

コードを読み取れない方や音声をダウンロードしたい方は、右のQRコードまたは以下のURLより、アクセスしてください。
https://www.mpi-j.co.jp/contents/shop/mpi/contents/digital/tagaki10.html

TAGAKI®10

発　行　日	●	2018年10月11日　初版第 1 刷　　2023年 1 月20日　第21刷
		2024年 3 月 1 日　 2 版第 2 刷
執　　　筆	●	松香洋子
執 筆 協 力	●	近藤理恵子
英 文 校 正	●	Glenn McDougall
編　　　集	●	株式会社カルチャー・プロ
イ ラ ス ト	●	池田蔵人　石井里果　小林昌子　サノエミコ　仲西太
本文デザイン・組版	●	DB Works
録 音 ・ 編 集	●	一般財団法人英語教育協議会（ELEC）
ナレーション	●	Erica Williams　Jon Mudryj　Julia Yermakov
写 真 提 供	●	法隆寺　便利堂　アフロ
協　　　力	●	赤松由梨　粕谷みゆき　貞野浩子　野中美恵　宮下いづみ　山内由紀子
印　　　刷	●	シナノ印刷株式会社
発　　　行	●	株式会社mpi松香フォニックス
		〒151-0053
		東京都渋谷区代々木2-16-2 第二甲田ビル 2F
		fax:03-5302-1652
		URL:https://www.mpi-j.co.jp

不許複製　All rights reserved.
©2018 mpi Matsuka Phonics inc.
ISBN 978-4-89643-745-4

＊本書で取り扱っている内容は、2017年までの情報をもとに作成しています。
＊QRコードは（株）デンソーウェーブの登録商標です。